When Robin Found Her Purpose

WRITTEN AND ILLUSTRATED

BY WENDY KEMP

DEDICATION

This book is dedicated to my mum
and everyone wishing to find white feathers.

A ROBIN APPEARS WHEN
A LOST LOVED ONE IS NEAR

Hi, I'm Rosie Robin; your friendly, reliable postie. I live in a beautiful home blanketed in sweet-smelling pink roses. It was inspired by Charles Rennie Mackintosh, as I love his *Rose* design. It is secretively hidden among the roses that cling to the wall of the grand Victorian house that you can see in the distance from where you live. From my residence, I can see every street in the town and I know the name of every person, animal and bird who lives here. My memory of places and names is a skill I acquired long before I started my job as a postie.

I have an instinctive sense of direction, which comes in handy when I get asked the way to Africa by the swallows each year before their grand migration.

My memory of people's names and where everyone lives is essential as a postie, especially when the writing on the letters is very difficult to read. I am quite sure that being a postie is my life's purpose.

Zen Master Kingfisher once told me that if
you want to find your purpose in life you
must listen to whatever your heart loves and
follow the path which shines most brightly.
I know that a lot of my friends are following
their callings.
Natasha Nuthatch is very talented. She loves
the violin and plays for the London Philharmonic Orchestra.

Burt Bullfinch is a genius with
numbers. He works in finance in the
City of London. Mrs Long Tail Tit
loves being a mother and nurturing
her family. It is a joy to watch her and
her chicks on their daily family outings. Her brood seem to want to
stay at home with her forever.

One of my favourite times as a postie was delivering love letters
from Mr Hare to Mrs Hare when he was away on business. Mrs
Hare kept all her letters tied in a large bow of pale blue satin
ribbon which she kept on her bedside table.

Mr Hare was an expert on soil and gave talks all over the world. His lectures taught how precious soil is, particularly when it comes to growing the best carrots. On his letters to Mrs Hare, he would attach the most interesting stamps. They showed or symbolised the places he was working. I would try and guess which country he was in by examining each intricate picture. I remember one of his stamps had an image of the most exotic birds you could ever imagine; birds with magnificently vibrant feathers. I remember wondering if he was writing from heaven!

Tragically, disaster struck one day. Mr Hare had a terrible accident and died, passing to the afterlife. This was a deeply sad time for everyone who knew him and he was greatly missed. He was a kind and gentle hare with such passion for protecting nature. He was driven to find and share ways to help our Earth. He had given talks about soil-health all over the world and had inspired many people and animals with his wisdom.

Mrs Hare was heartbroken and one day her grief sent her to Master Kingfisher. With her, she took some freshly-baked scones, which had all the animals' noses twitching from the amazing scent in the air. She also took some of his favourite green tea.

When she arrived, they sat together for a while, drinking tea without saying a word. Mrs Hare knew that he would give her guidance as Master Kingfisher was known for his superb wisdom on all matters. His spiritual insight seemed to enable him to always say the right thing. He took a tiny sip of tea from his emerald green cup. Then he turned to her and spoke. He explained that finding stillness and acceptance would help her grief. If she could be still and learn to empty her mind of unhelpful thoughts, she would be able to feel the love pouring into her heart from her husband. She left with hope and felt much calmer. Everyone always felt better after their visits with Zen Master Kingfisher.

After her tea with Master Kingfisher, Mrs Hare went to the top of Big Hill to try and sit in stillness and silence. In the weeks that followed, she routinely sat there every day for twenty minutes, gazing up at the sky. Determined to quieten her mind, she waited patiently for some kind of message of love from her husband. Every time her mind began thinking unhelpful thoughts, she imagined these thoughts as clouds, passing and disappearing into the distance, leaving behind a clear blue sky.

I passed Mrs Hare every day on my rounds and she would say how hard it was to empty her mind of thoughts; her mind and heart felt so heavy with sadness. She told me how she longed for some kind of sign or confirmation that Mr Hare was at peace in the afterlife. I always left feeling so sad for her and wishing there was something I could do to help.

My closest and dearest of friends is Felix Fox. He is a philatelist (pronounced fil-at-ol-ist). This is the name given to someone who collects stamps. In fact, it was Felix's passion about stamps that inspired me to like stamps too. You should see Felix's home. The walls are decorated from top to bottom in a diverse array of stamps. He has collected them from Australia, Egypt, Africa and all over the world. He has some which date back hundreds of years.

My favourite thing about stamps is that they remind me of tiny intricate paintings. Their designs and images never cease to interest me, and the frilly white part reminds me of a frame going around a painting. Felix and I often sit for hours with our magnifying glasses, studying the fine details. Over the years we must have seen thousands of these little four-sided treasures.
As a matter of fact, it was a stamp that almost caused my death.

Every day, Rory Rooster wakes me up very early. When it's still very dark, I get up, I shake my feathers and set off on my rounds to deliver letters and packages to the people, birds and animals in town.

One particularly chilly morning, there was such a cloudless, dark sky that the stars twinkled more brightly than ever. I filled my bag with the first batch of letters and set off with a merry tune. It had snowed in the night and I was the first bird to make prints in the snow. I reached into the bag and pulled out the first letter. Before I looked at the name and address, I was immediately drawn to the stamp. I was sure this was one of the stamps that Felix had told me about a couple of years ago. It was made in 1918 and I remember it clearly because it was a picture of a plane, which was first used by the post office to carry mail. I recognised the bright red words *U.S. Postage* which surrounded the tiny image of the dark indigo plane. I fluttered excitedly and exclaimed, "Oh! I must find Felix!"

I flew as fast as my wings would carry me, my heavy bag of mail by my side. I was feeling rather dizzy so I stopped for a rest and to catch my breath outside Barnaby Blue Tit's house. I looked again at the letter and scanned for the address.

"Oh, that's good," I said, feeling quite relieved. "It's addressed to Felix."

Looking again at the stamp, while catching my breath, something didn't quite make sense. I scratched my head and pondered. Then I realised that the picture of the plane was upside down. Felix had once told me about misprinted stamps. These, he had explained, were incredibly rare and some stamp collectors would pay huge amounts of money for them. Excitedly, I put the letter back in the bag, fastened it and flung it over my shoulder. Felix's house was just around the next corner.

Felix was coming out of the woods on the edge of town. He had been taking an early stroll in the quiet of morning. He saw me flying around the corner and called out to me, "Hey, Rosie! Have you seen the sky?"

I looked up and saw the most beautiful sky I had ever seen. It was filled with a glowing green light called the aurora borealis. I simply couldn't take my eyes off it. Bright green waves of light moved like swishing curtains, dancing gracefully above me. I had never seen anything like it before. This had to be the best day ever…

The next thing I remember was being at Folly. Folly was the local bird and animal hospital. Felix had watched me fly straight into a tree whilst being distracted by the beautiful aurora. He had picked me up and carried me to Folly straight away.

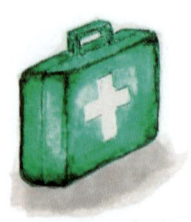

The next part of my story is very important, and you must remember it always.

I had never experienced this in my life, but my soul had actually left my body. I could see my limp form, lying on a table. Felix was holding my wing while people attached their special machines, very gently, to my chest. It was almost as if I was watching a movie of myself. I seemed to be floating in the air, looking down upon my physical body below. There was a bit of commotion among the people and then I drifted upwards. It was such a lovely peaceful feeling.

I thought to myself, "I must be dead," but it didn't frighten me. Quite the opposite in fact. I could see a warm glow and was drawn towards it. As I moved closer, I could feel a love so powerful. It was complete bliss! I can only describe this love as being like the love you feel for your newborn. I was so calm and happy. There was so much love; so much peace. I had entered a higher realm of existence.

I remember moving into this glow and being surrounded by incredible golden light beings. Right before me stood breathtakingly beautiful angels with their magnificent wings. The feeling of love only deepened as they spoke to me. They didn't talk out loud but I just knew what they were saying. We were communicating with our minds, telepathically. Things happened differently and it is far too complicated for my little brain to explain now, but at the time when I was there, it all made perfect sense.

I was then met by another angel, who had a different coloured light-energy. This angel was surrounded by an enchanting purple glow. There must have been so many questions, flying around in my head, and they answered each one in turn. I asked, "Does everyone see angels when they die?"

They explained to me that they are a frequency and energy beyond our understanding. They can manifest in different ways, according to the person's religious, spiritual or non-spiritual beliefs. They manifested into angels for me because of our connection to feathers.

"Yesterday, I was a Buddha. The day before, I was Allah. The day before that, I was Jesus," an angel explained, in the simplest way she could.

"Of course. That all makes sense now," I nodded, thanking them.

In the next instant, I was watching my life's review. It was like watching a film where I was the lead role. I could see the moment I was born and the time I was mean to my brother when we fought over a worm in a garden. I could see how hard I worked at school and my kind deeds, like looking after Felix when he had broken his nose the time he fell, doing cartwheels, down Big Hill. I saw how I tried to make him laugh by sticking one of his stamps to my forehead, which turned into a game of Guess Who. All of my lifetime on Earth, as Rosie Robin, was shown to me. It felt like I had just had an instant download of all my life and it was shown with no timeline but given to me all at once.

I remember back on earth seeing little stamps with religious paintings called 'The Day of Judgement'. I realised that there was no external being judging the life I had led. It was my mind that judged itself, as I saw my whole life play out. On the whole I'd had an amazing life and done some incredible things, had fun, been kind and learned lots of lessons.

A different angel guided me on to another place. It was as if, in the blink of an eye, I was transported to the most paradisaic garden you had ever seen. Words cannot describe the colours and light – you had to be there to see it for yourself. The love, beauty and peace were indescribable. I could hear the butterflies' wings resonating like a purr. I wanted to stay forever. I had never felt so much peace. And I was not alone. I was surrounded by people, birds and animals that I had known, who had died. They were so happy and what I can only describe as lighter and freer. They were emanating such tranquillity and love that I wanted to be still and immerse myself in this perfection, always.

I wondered if Mr Hare was there. Then, just as the thought entered my head, he appeared right in front of me.

"Rosie," he said, telepathically. I could feel so much warmth, being in Mr Hare's presence. He told me that his life review went very well. His soul was happy with all he had learned and had achieved on Earth and he had successfully completed his soul contract. He told me that he and the council in heaven were deciding on his next life. He had not yet reached enlightenment and he had more lessons to learn on Earth. His soul needed to grow and he had to go back to Earth with a new purpose. In his next lifetime he was going to be a human being. His purpose was to use his skills to manage many acres of land in a way which would help the environment. He was excited about going back to Earth so he could help to make the world a better place. But before he could start a new life, he wanted to watch over Mrs Hare and send her love. He asked me about my soul contract; I didn't really know what he meant so I just shrugged my wings.

"Rosie!" called another friendly voice that I recognised. "You are not supposed to have died just yet."

It was Bodhi Blue Tit. Bodhi was a dear friend of mine who was killed by Gertrude Great Tit. When Bodhi was in Earth School she never judged and had the biggest heart for everyone and anyone. Above all, she was kind and always found herself involved in some sort of project for humanity or the environment. We all called her an Earth Angel.

She said she was very content and at peace in this heavenly plane and enjoyed her work in guiding Earth-beings. She was giving angelic guidance to Barnaby, her husband, and to her daughter, Belle, down in Earth School. She told me how they often ask for help and guidance with Earthly situations. She answers by making coincidences happen or by sending messages. Quite often, Bodhi sent a message via my cousin, Ruby Robin, by delivering a white feather to both Barnaby and Belle, as a reminder that she was watching over them, letting them know she was in a place of divine love.

When I heard this, something inside me twitched and tingled. This was the first physical sensation I had felt since being in this heavenly place.

Yet in the beat of a hummingbird's wing, I was back again in front of the beautiful, golden, glowing angels, once again. They had reviewed my soul contract. I learnt that we all have a soul contract before we are born which we have to fulfil in our life on Earth. They told me I had to go back to Earth because I had unfinished work to do. I had not completed my purpose. My purpose was to *Spread The Message.* At that moment, I really didn't want to go back. I'd never felt so happy, so at peace or such intense love as I did here in this heavenly plane.

There was no discussion. In a flash, I was back in my body again. It felt so heavy and a shock of pain coursed through my head. I opened my eyes and took in the faces of the creatures around me. They looked overjoyed! Felix was crying with happiness upon seeing that I was alive.

I couldn't believe that I had died, gone to the afterlife and come back to Earth again. I had no concept of time. I could have been dead for days, hours, minutes or seconds.

As I lay recovering in bed over the next few days, I pondered what the angels meant when they said I had "unfinished business" to do and that I was to "spread the message". Carefully, I stepped out of bed and onto the floor. Then, from nowhere, there appeared a little white feather. I picked it up and held it gently. A memory of the sense of love from my time in the afterlife came back to me. Then I heard a voice. It was Mr Hare!

"Rosie, please can you deliver this to Mrs Hare today? I want her to know I'm at peace and that I'm watching over her."

Then it came to me. I would be a messenger. A messenger of love. I would deliver white feathers to all the people who had lost loved ones. I would tell them never to worry about their loved ones who have passed over, as they really are in the most heavenly state of being.

I couldn't wait to get to work. As soon as I had recovered, I filled my bag with letters and packages, and kept a special place for white feathers. My first stop was to go and see Mrs Hare, to deliver my first white feather. I went to the top of Big Hill, where she often sat gazing up at the sky. She hadn't yet arrived. I took the beautiful white feather out of my bag and laid it amongst the dandelions.

"She will find that soon," I whispered to myself and flew off, brimming with happiness. I could sense the angels smiling down at me.

"Thank you," said Mr Hare, from above.

From that moment on, I was busy receiving messages from people who had died and delivering white feathers. I had found my purpose! This work made my heart feel so full and I loved my job now, even more than ever.

THE END

'A message of LOVE is a feather from above'

In case you're wondering what happened to Felix, he went to see someone about that stamp with the upside-down plane on it. It turns out that it was called an 'Inverted Jenny' and was worth thousands of pounds. He sold it and used the money to buy a Post Office. He too has found a job he loves.

Other books written and illustrated By Wendy Kemp

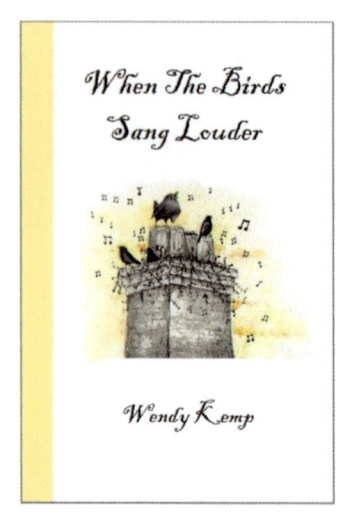

'When The Birds Sang Louder'
Blackbird tells his story about
the covid pandemic from his
wise perspective.

'Blue Tit's Visit To Ukraine'
Barnaby Blue Tit tells his story
about love, loss, compassion
and kindness.

In this inspiring story, Sid Seagull
takes us on his surprising journey to
find his true self and enlightenment.

ALL BOOKS ARE
AVAILABLE TO PURCHASE
FROM AMAZON

ABOUT THE AUTHOR

This book was inspired from Wendy's jewellery collections.

WWW.WENDYKEMPJEWELLERY.CO.UK

Printed in Great Britain
by Amazon

57820984R00025